*Congressional*
*Research*
*Service*

# Community Services Block Grants (CSBG): Background and Funding

Karen Spar
Specialist in Domestic Social Policy and Division Research Coordinator

November 19, 2013

Congressional Research Service

7-5700

www.crs.gov

RL32872

CRS Report for Congress ───────────────────────
*Prepared for Members and Committees of Congress*

# Summary

Community Services Block Grants (CSBG) provide federal funds to states, territories, and tribes for distribution to local agencies to support a wide range of community-based activities to reduce poverty. Smaller related programs—Community Economic Development (CED), Rural Community Facilities (RCF), and Individual Development Accounts (IDAs)—also support anti-poverty efforts. CSBG and some of these related activities trace their roots to the War on Poverty, launched in the 1960s. Today, they are administered at the federal level by the Department of Health and Human Services (HHS).

CSBG and related activities are currently funded through January 15, 2014, under an interim continuing resolution (P.L. 113-46) that generally maintains funding at FY2013 levels, including certain reductions made as a result of the March 1, 2013, budget sequestration and an across-the-board rescission required to keep discretionary spending within statutory limits. Full-year FY2013 funding was provided by P.L. 113-6 and generally maintained funding at FY2012 levels, reduced by sequestration and the across-the-board rescission.

After making the reductions, HHS announced that FY2013 funding levels for CSBG and related activities totaled $687 million, including $635 million for the block grant, $28 million for CED, $5 million for RCF, and almost $19 million for IDAs. This compared with a total of $732 million in FY2012, including $677 million for the block grant, $30 million for CED, $5 million for RCF, and $20 million for IDAs.

President Obama submitted his FY2014 budget to Congress on April 10, 2013, proposing $350 million for CSBG, $19.5 million for IDAs, and zero for other related activities. The request for CSBG marked a sharp drop from recent funding levels, although the Administration made the same request for FY2012 and FY2013 and Congress rejected the proposal both times. The FY2014 budget marked the first time the Administration proposed terminating the CED program. However, it would continue funding the Healthy Food Financing Initiative (which has been partially financed with CED funds) through a Treasury Department program. The White House previously proposed eliminating RCF, but Congress has continued to provide funding each year.

In previous budgets, the Obama Administration has signaled its intent to move CSBG toward a competitive program, in which states would direct funds toward local agencies that meet certain standards, rather than via the current mandatory pass-through to all "eligible entities." The Administration's FY2014 budget reiterated this intent, stating that HHS would work with Congress to develop "core" federal standards to measure local performance. If an eligible entity failed to meet these standards, the state would conduct an open competition to replace that entity.

The National Association for State Community Services Programs conducts an annual survey of states on the activities and expenditures of the nationwide network of more than 1,000 CSBG grantees. According to the most recent survey, the network served more than 16 million people in almost 7 million low-income families in FY2012. States reported that the network spent $14.5 billion of federal, state, local, and private resources, including $610 million of regular federal CSBG funds and more than $10 billion from other federal programs.

The Community Services Block Grant Act was last reauthorized in 1998 by P.L. 105-285. The authorization of appropriations for CSBG and most related programs expired in FY2003, although Congress has continued to fund these programs through annual appropriations. No legislation to reauthorize CSBG has been introduced since the 109th Congress.

# Contents

# Appendixes

# Contacts

# Recent Developments

## FY2014 Funding

The Community Services Block Grant (CSBG) and related activities are currently funded through January 15, 2014, under an interim continuing resolution (P.L. 113-46) that generally maintains discretionary programs at FY2013 levels, including certain reductions that were made in FY2013. These reductions—from FY2012 levels—were the result of a budget "sequestration" that took effect on March 1, 2013, and an across-the-board rescission determined necessary by the Office of Management and Budget (OMB) to keep discretionary spending within statutory limits.

For FY2013, the Department of Health and Human Services (HHS) published an "all-purpose table" that presents funding levels for agency programs after the reductions were made. The table shows a combined total of $687 million for CSBG and related activities in FY2013, including $635 million for the CSBG, $28 million for Community Economic Development (CED), $5 million for Rural Community Facilities (RCF), and almost $19 million for Individual Development Accounts (IDAs) under the Assets for Independence (AFI) program. Presumably, these are the amounts in effect through January 15, 2014, under P.L. 113-46. However, the full-year FY2014 budget and appropriations process is not complete as of this writing.

"Sequestration" is an automatic across-the-board spending reduction process under which budgetary resources are permanently canceled to enforce certain budget policy goals. Under the Budget Control Act of 2011 (P.L. 112-25), OMB was directed to implement automatic budget enforcement procedures, including sequestration, for each of FY2013 through FY2021 to enforce deficit reduction goals. The FY2013 sequestration originally was scheduled to occur on January 2, 2013, but was postponed by the American Taxpayer Relief Act (P.L. 112-240) until March 1, 2013, when OMB announced that nondefense discretionary programs (such as CSBG and related activities) would be subject to a 5% reduction. OMB further announced on April 4 that an across-the-board rescission of 0.2% would be necessary to avoid a breach of statutory limits on discretionary spending for FY2013. For more information on FY2014 funding, see "Funding and Legislative Proposals for FY2014."

## FY2014 Budget Request

The Obama Administration submitted its FY2014 budget to Congress on April 10, 2013, requesting $350 million for the CSBG and $19.5 million for Individual Development Accounts. Nothing was requested for the other two currently funded related activities: Community Economic Development and Rural Community Facilities. Under current appropriations law, the Administration's Healthy Food Financing Initiative receives a carve-out of funding through the CED program; however, for FY2014 the Administration requested this funding through a Treasury Department program. For more details, see "Administration Proposal," later in this report. Also see **Table 1** for a comparison of proposed FY2014 funding with amounts provided in FY2013 and previous years.

# Background

Administered by the Department of Health and Human Services (HHS), the Community Services Block Grant (CSBG) program provides federal funds to states, territories, and Indian tribes for distribution to local agencies in support of a variety of antipoverty activities. The origins of the Community Services Block Grant date back to 1964, when the Economic Opportunity Act (P.L. 88-452; 42 U.S.C. §2701) established the War on Poverty and authorized the Office of Economic Opportunity (OEO) as the lead agency in the federal antipoverty campaign. A centerpiece of OEO was the Community Action Program, under which a nationwide network of local Community Action Agencies (CAAs) was developed. A key feature of Community Action is the direct involvement of low-income people in the design and administration of antipoverty activities, through mandatory representation on the CAAs' governing boards. Currently, at the local level, CAAs are the primary grantees of the CSBG.

In 1975, OEO was renamed the Community Services Administration (CSA), but remained an independent executive branch agency. In 1981, CSA was abolished and replaced by the CSBG, to be administered by HHS. At the time CSA was abolished, it was administering nearly 900 CAAs, about 40 local community development corporations, and several small categorical programs that were typically operated by local CAAs. The CSBG Act was enacted as part of the Omnibus Budget Reconciliation Act of 1981 (P.L. 97-35, Title VI, §671; 42 U.S.C. §9901) as partial response to President Reagan's proposal to consolidate CSA with 11 other social service programs into a block grant to states. Congress rejected this proposal and instead created two new block grants, the Social Services Block Grant under Title XX of the Social Security Act, and the CSBG, which consisted of activities previously administered by CSA.

The CSBG Act was reauthorized in 1984 under P.L. 98-558, in 1986 under P.L. 99-425, in 1990 under P.L. 101-501, in 1994 under P.L. 103-252, and in 1998 under P.L. 105-285. The authorization of appropriations for CSBG and most related programs expired in FY2003. The House and Senate passed reauthorization legislation during the 108th Congress but it was not enacted. Similar legislation was introduced in the 109th Congress but not considered. No legislation to reauthorize CSBG has been introduced since the 109th Congress.

Several related national activities—Community Economic Development (CED), Rural Community Facilities (RCF), and Individual Development Accounts (IDAs)—currently receive appropriations separate from the block grant and offer grants to assist local low-income communities with economic development, rural housing and water management, and asset development for low-income individuals. These activities are administered at the federal level by the same Office of Community Services at HHS (part of the Administration for Children and Families) that administers the CSBG, and in some cases, are also authorized by the CSBG Act. Prior to FY2012, a related activity called Job Opportunities for Low-Income Individuals (JOLI) received a separate appropriation, and prior to FY2006, national activities that received separate appropriations also included the National Youth Sports and Community Food and Nutrition programs.

## The Block Grant[1]

### Allocation of Funds

Of funds appropriated annually under the CSBG Act, HHS is required to reserve 1.5% for training and technical assistance and other administrative activities, and half of this set-aside must be provided to state or local entities. In addition, 0.5% of the appropriation is reserved for outlying territories (Guam, American Samoa, the Virgin Islands, and the Northern Mariana Islands). The law further requires that 9% of the total appropriation be reserved for certain related activities, which are described below, and that the remainder be allocated among the states. In practice, however, Congress typically specifies in annual appropriations laws exactly how much is to be made available for the block grant and each of the related activities. Block grant funds are allotted to states (including Puerto Rico) based on the relative amount received in each state, in FY1981, under a section of the former Economic Opportunity Act. HHS may allow Indian tribes to receive their allotments directly, rather than through the state.

### Use of Funds

CSBG funds are used for activities designed to have a "measurable and potentially major impact on causes of poverty." The law envisions a wide variety of activities undertaken on behalf of low-income families and individuals, including those who are welfare recipients, homeless, migrant or seasonal farm workers, or elderly. States must submit an application and plan to HHS, stating their intention that funds will be used for activities to help families and individuals achieve self-sufficiency, find and retain meaningful employment, attain an adequate education, make better use of available income, obtain adequate housing, and achieve greater participation in community affairs. In addition, states must ensure that funds will be used to address the needs of youth in low-income communities; coordinate with related programs, including state welfare reform efforts; and ensure that local grantees provide emergency food-related services.

### State Role

At the state level, a lead agency must be designated to develop the state application and plan. States must pass through at least 90% of their federal CSBG allotment to local eligible entities.[2] States also may use up to $55,000 or 5% of their allotment, whichever is higher, for administrative costs.[3] Remaining funds may be used by the state to provide training and technical assistance, coordination and communication activities, payments to assure that funds are targeted to areas with the greatest need, supporting "asset-building" programs for low-income individuals (such as Individual Development Accounts, discussed later), supporting innovative programs and activities conducted by local organizations, or other activities consistent with the purposes of the

---

[1] See **Table 2** for a history of CSBG appropriations from its first year of funding (FY1982) through FY2013.

[2] Under a one-time appropriation of $1 billion for the CSBG under the American Recovery and Reinvestment Act (ARRA, P.L. 111-5), states were required to pass through 99% of their allotments to local eligible entities and use the remaining 1% for benefits eligibility coordination activities. See "American Recovery and Reinvestment Act of 2009," later in this report.

[3] The Urban Institute has conducted an evaluation of the use of CSBG administrative funds, published in February 2012, which is available at http://www.urban.org/UploadedPDF/412601-Community-Services-Block-Grant-Administrative-Expenses.pdf.

CSBG Act. In addition, as authorized by the 1998 amendments, states may use some CSBG funds to offset revenue losses associated with any qualified state charity tax credit.

## Local Delivery System

As noted above, states are required to pass through at least 90% of their federal block grant allotments to "eligible entities"—primarily (but not exclusively) Community Action Agencies (CAAs) that had been designated prior to 1981 under the former Economic Opportunity Act. The distribution of these funds among local agencies is left to the discretion of the state, although states may not terminate funding to an eligible entity or reduce its share disproportionately without determining cause, after notice and an opportunity for a hearing. There are more than 1,000 eligible entities around the country, the majority of which are private nonprofit organizations. Many of these organizations contract with others in delivering various services. Once designated as an eligible entity for a particular community, an agency retains its designation unless it voluntarily withdraws from the program or its grant is terminated for cause. Eligible entities are monitored within a systematic schedule; return visits are made when goals are not met. In designating new or replacement entities, states may select a public agency only when no qualified private nonprofit organization is available, in accordance with the 1998 CSBG amendments.

Local activities vary depending on the needs and circumstances of the local community. Each eligible entity, or CAA, is governed by a board of directors, of which at least one-third are representatives of the low-income community. Under the 1998 amendments to the CSBG Act, low-income board members must live in the community that they represent. Another third of the board members must be local elected officials or their representatives, and the remaining board members represent other community interests, such as business, labor, religious organizations, and education. A public entity must either have a governing board with low-income representation as described above, or another mechanism specified by the state to assure participation by low-income individuals in the development, planning, implementation, and evaluation of programs.

There is no typical CAA, since each agency designs its programs based on a local community needs assessment. Examples, however, of CSBG-funded services include emergency assistance, home weatherization, activities for youth and senior citizens, transportation, income management and credit counseling, domestic violence crisis assistance, parenting education, food pantries, and emergency shelters. In addition, local agencies provide information and referral to other community services, such as job training and vocational education, depending on the needs of individual clients.

# Currently Funded Related Activities

In addition to the block grant itself, the CSBG Act authorizes several related national activities that are currently funded and administered through the Office of Community Services within HHS. Individual Development Accounts are not directly authorized by the CSBG Act, but are also administered by the Office of Community Services.[4] Funding authorization for the following

---

[4] The Office of Community Services administers several additional programs; however, these are not considered part of the cluster of CSBG-related activities and are not discussed in this report. These programs include the Social Services Block Grant, the Low-Income Home Energy Assistance Program (LIHEAP), and the Strengthening Communities (continued...)

activities expired at the end of FY2003; however, Congress has continued to fund them through the annual appropriations process (see **Table 1**).

## Community Economic Development[5]

The Community Economic Development (CED) program helps support local community development corporations (CDCs) to generate employment and business development opportunities for low-income residents. Projects must directly benefit persons living at or below the poverty level and must be completed within 12 to 60 months of the date the grant was awarded. Preferred projects are those that document public/private partnership, including the leveraging of cash and in-kind contributions; and those that are located in areas characterized by poverty, a Temporary Assistance for Needy Families (TANF) assistance rate of at least 20%, high levels of unemployment or incidences of violence, gang activity, and other indicators of socioeconomic distress.

During FY2012, HHS supported 38 grants, of which all were new starts, plus five contracts and one interagency agreement, according to agency budget documents. This was an increase in the number of grantees from FY2011, when the program supported 25 grants (all new starts), plus six contracts and one interagency agreement. For FY2013, the department expected to support 35 grants, of which all would be new starts, plus four contracts and one interagency agreement. No program activity is projected for CED in FY2014, as the Administration requested no continued funding for this program.

### *Healthy Food Financing Initiative[6]*

The Healthy Food Financing Initiative (HFFI) is a multiyear multiagency effort through which HHS has partnered with the Departments of Agriculture (USDA) and the Treasury to make available a total of $400 million to address the lack of affordable healthy food in many urban and rural communities (areas known as "food deserts"). Under the HHS/CED component, competitive grants go to community development corporations for projects to finance grocery stores, farmers markets, and other sources of fresh nutritious food, creating employment and business opportunities in low-income communities while also providing access to healthy food options. Legislation that would formally authorize the program in USDA was proposed in the 112th Congress and is pending in the 113th Congress, in the Senate version of the "farm bill" (S. 954).[7]

In each of its budget submissions for FY2011 through FY2013, the Administration proposed that a certain amount of CED funding be dedicated toward the HFFI. For FY2012, Congress reserved $10 million of CED funding for this initiative, and the Administration requested the same level for FY2013. For FY2014, the Administration proposed no funding for HFFI through the CED

---

(...continued)
Initiative.

[5] For more information on this program, see http://www.acf.hhs.gov/programs/ocs/programs/ced.

[6] For more information about this program, see http://www.acf.hhs.gov/programs/ocs/programs/community-economic-development/healthy-food-financing. Also see discussion of HFFI in CRS Report R42155, *The Role of Local Food Systems in U.S. Farm Policy*, by Renée Johnson, Randy Alison Aussenberg, and Tadlock Cowan.

[7] See discussion of nutrition provisions in CRS Report R43076, *The 2013 Farm Bill: A Comparison of the Senate-Passed (S. 954) and House-Passed (H.R. 2642, H.R. 3102) Bills with Current Law*, coordinated by Ralph M. Chite.

program; instead, $10 million for HFFI was requested through the Treasury Department's Community Development Financial Institutions program. According to HHS budget documents, the Administration for Children and Families (which administers CSBG and related programs through its Office of Community Services) will continue to collaborate with the Treasury Department on the HFFI initiative.

## Rural Community Facilities[8]

Funds are for grants to public and private nonprofit organizations for rural housing and community facilities development projects to train and offer technical assistance on the following: home repair to low-income families, water and waste water facilities management, and developing low-income rental housing units. Each year beginning with its FY2010 budget request to Congress, the Obama Administration has proposed to terminate this program, arguing that it does not belong in HHS. Instead, the Administration noted that federal assistance for water treatment facilities is available through two much larger programs in the Environmental Protection Agency (EPA) (i.e., the Clean Water and Drinking Water State Revolving Funds) and through direct loans, loan guarantees, and grants administered by the Department of Agriculture (USDA).

During FY2012, HHS supported eight grants, all of which were continuation grants, plus one contract and one interagency agreement, according to agency budget documents. In FY2013, the department expected to maintain the same level of activity. HHS expects no program activity in FY2014 due to the program's proposed termination.

## Individual Development Accounts[9]

The Assets for Independence Act (AFI, Title IV, P.L. 105-285) initially authorized a five-year demonstration initiative to encourage low-income people to accumulate savings. Individual Development Accounts (IDAs) are dedicated savings accounts that can be used for specific purposes, such as buying a first home, paying for college, or starting a business. Contributions are matched, and participants are given financial and investment counseling. To conduct the demonstration, grants are made to public or private nonprofit organizations that can raise an amount of private and public (nonfederal) funds that is equal to the federal grant; federal matches into IDA cannot exceed the non-federal matches. The maximum federal grant is $1 million a year, and HHS says the average grant is currently about $286,000.

In budget documents, HHS notes that it has established a performance-based approach to administering this program. Critical performance measures include the amount of earned income participants withdraw from their IDAs to make allowable purchases (e.g., for a home, higher education, or small business) and the number of participants who make such withdrawals. These

---

[8] For more information about this program, also known as the Rural Community Development Program, see http://www.acf.hhs.gov/programs/ocs/programs/rcd.

[9] For more information on this program, see http://www.acf.hhs.gov/programs/ocs/programs/afi. Also see CRS Report RS22185, *Individual Development Accounts (IDAs): Background on Federal Grant Programs to Help Low-Income Families Save*, by Gene Falk; and the most recent annual report to Congress on the program by HHS, "Assets for Independence Program: Status at the Conclusion of the Eleventh Year," available at http://www.acf.hhs.gov/sites/default/files/ocs/11th_afi_report_to_congress.pdf.

measures have generally shown improvement since FY2005, including for the most recent year (FY2011) for which results are available.

The Assets for Independence Act expired at the end of FY2003, although Congress has continued to provide appropriations for the IDA program under this authority. In HHS budget documents for FY2014, the Administration stated its intention to work with Congress to reauthorize and amend the program to

> advance continued knowledge development, promote flexibility and simplify program administration by: (1) providing grantees more flexibility in project administration; (2) authorizing the Secretary to waive statutory provisions and test new approaches; (3) reducing the amount of non-federal match requirement that AFI grantees are required to meet; (4) making permanent the authority to recapture and reallocate any AFI grant funds that have not been expended by qualified entities; and granting the Secretary authority to utilize up to $1,000,000 annually to support high quality program research and evaluation.[10]

According to Administration budget documents, in FY2012 the program supported 61 new grants, 10 contracts, and one interagency agreement. HHS expected to support 47 new grants, 10 contracts, and one interagency agreement in FY2013, and to maintain approximately this same level in FY2014. In the first phase of its national evaluation of the program, HHS reported that participants derived substantial benefits and were more likely than comparable non-participants to become homeowners or business owners and to pursue postsecondary education.[11]

Legislation has been introduced in the 113th Congress (H.R. 2110) that would amend and reauthorize appropriations for this program at an annual level of $75 million for FY2014 through FY2018. The bill is currently pending before the House Ways and Means Committee.

## Formerly Funded Related Activities

Three additional related national activities were funded in earlier years. These include the National Youth Sports Program and Community Food and Nutrition Program, both authorized under the CSBG Act, and Job Opportunities for Low-Income Individuals (JOLI), which was not authorized by the CSBG Act but was administered as a related activity by the Office of Community Services. Funding authorization for these activities expired at the end of FY2003, with the exception of JOLI, which is permanently authorized.

### National Youth Sports Program

Under this program, a grant traditionally was made to a single organization, namely the National Collegiate Athletic Association (NCAA), to provide recreational and instructional services for low-income youth, typically on college campuses. In FY2005, Congress appropriated $18 million for this program, and one award was made. No direct federal funding has been provided since that year. Legislation was introduced in the 112th Congress (H.R. 2817 and §302 of H.R. 2795) to reauthorize appropriations for this program at an annual level of $20 million for FY2012 through

---

[10] See Administration for Children and Families, Fiscal Year 2014, Justification of Estimates for Appropriations Committees, https://www.acf hhs.gov/sites/default/files/olab/fy_2014_cj_final_web.pdf, page 181.

[11] See process and impact studies from the national evaluation of Assets for Independence, available at http://www.acf.hhs.gov/programs/ocs/resource/afi-program-evaluation.

FY2022 (or through FY2021 in H.R. 2795). This proposal also was introduced in the 111th Congress (H.R. 4480).

### Community Food and Nutrition Program

This program authorized grants to public and private nonprofit organizations to coordinate food assistance resources, to help identify potential sponsors of child nutrition programs and to initiate programs in areas with inadequate food assistance resources, and to develop innovative approaches at the state and local level to meet the nutritional needs of low-income people. Authorizing legislation required that 60% of the amount appropriated (up to $6 million) must be allocated to states for statewide programs and that 40% must be awarded on a competitive basis. Amounts appropriated in excess of $6 million were allotted as follows: 40% awarded to eligible agencies for statewide grants; 40% awarded on a competitive basis for local and statewide programs; and 20% awarded on a competitive basis for nationwide programs, including programs benefitting Native Americans and migrant farm workers. For FY2005, Congress appropriated $7 million for this program; no funding has been provided since then.

### Job Opportunities for Low-Income Individuals (JOLI)[12]

JOLI is permanently authorized under the Family Support Act of 1988 (P.L. 100-485, §505), as amended by the Personal Responsibility and Work Opportunity Reconciliation Act of 1996 (P.L. 104-193, §112). Although JOLI is not authorized under the CSBG Act, it was funded and administered as one of the CSBG-related activities; however, it has not been funded since FY2011 when it received less than $2 million. JOLI funds were awarded on a competitive basis to community based, non-profit, and tax-exempt organizations, including community development corporations, faith-based, charitable, and tribal organizations. Organizations awarded grants were required to demonstrate and evaluate ways of creating new employment opportunities with private employers for individuals who received TANF and for other individuals whose family income level did not exceed 100% of the official poverty guidelines. Examples of these projects included self-employment and micro-enterprise, new businesses, expansion of existing businesses, or creating new jobs or employment opportunities. Funds for this project could not be used for new construction or for the purchase of real property.

## CSBG Program Data

The *Community Services Block Grant Annual Report FY2013* summarizes data for FY2012 submitted by 50 states, the District of Columbia, and Puerto Rico in response to the most recent annual survey funded by HHS and administered by the National Association for State Community Services Programs.[13] According to this report, the nationwide CSBG network consisted of 1,045 local eligible entities in FY2012, including 919 Community Action Agencies, 84 local government agencies, 17 "limited purpose agencies" that specialized in one or two types of

---

[12] For more information about this program, see http://www.acf hhs.gov/programs/ocs/programs/joli.

[13] *Community Services Block Grant Annual Report FY2013*, National Association for State Community Services Programs, Washington, DC, September 2013, available at http://www nascsp.org/data/files/csbg_publications/annual_reports/reports/2013report-full-report-final.pdf

programs, 17 tribes or tribal organizations,[14] five migrant or seasonal farmworker organizations, and three organizations that fell into other categories.

This network of local eligible entities reported spending $14.5 billion in FY2012, with funding coming from federal, state, local, and private sources. Of the total amount spent, $610 million came from the federal CSBG allotment. Nearly $10 billion of the funding spent by local entities in FY2012 came from federal programs—*other than CSBG*—and of that total, almost $630 million was originally appropriated through the American Recovery and Reinvestment Act (ARRA, P.L. 111-5). More than $1.5 billion came from state governments, more than $1.3 billion came from private agencies, and nearly $1 billion came from local governments.

## Use of Federal CSBG Funds

Based on reports from all jurisdictions, local entities spent their regular CSBG funds in FY2012 for a wide variety of activities, including emergency services (19%); activities to promote self-sufficiency (17%); activities to promote linkages among community groups and other government or private organizations (13%); education-related activities (12%); employment-related activities (11%); housing-related services (8%); nutrition services (6%); income management (6%); health services (5%); and other activities.

## Sources of Federal Non-CSBG Funds

The bulk of funds spent by local eligible entities come from federal programs other than CSBG. Of $9.1 billion in non-CSBG non-ARRA federal funds spent by local agencies in FY2012, 33% came from Head Start or Early Head Start, and 20% came from the Low-Income Home Energy Assistance Program (LIHEAP).

States reported that almost 6% of federal (non-CSBG non-ARRA) funds received by local agencies came from the TANF block grant; almost 4% came from employment and training programs administered by the Labor Department; almost 3% came from the Department of Housing and Urban Development (HUD) Section 8 assisted housing program; and almost 3% came from the Child Care and Development Block Grant. The following each accounted for more than 2% of spending in FY2012 by local eligible entities: the Department of Energy's weatherization program; the Department of Agriculture's Special Supplemental Nutrition Program for Women, Infants and Children (WIC); and HUD's Community Development Block Grant. Medicare and Medicaid combined accounted for nearly 2%.

## Recipients of CSBG Services

According to states responding to the survey, the CSBG network provided services to more than 16 million individuals in 6.9 million families in FY2012. Of families for whom the survey captured demographic information, nearly 70% had incomes at or below federal poverty

---

[14] Tribes and tribal organizations may participate in the CSBG program as local eligible entities. In addition, tribes may request to receive funds directly from HHS, rather than through the state in which they are located. In the first quarter of FY2014, 60 individual tribes or tribal organizations received direct allotments from HHS. These amounts were subtracted from the allotments of states in which the tribal or tribal organization was located. See http://www.acf.hhs.gov/sites/default/files/ocs/fy2014_csbg_1st_quarter_allocations_0.pdf

guidelines and a third of families were "severely poor" with incomes at or below 50% of the poverty guidelines. More than 87% of families that reported some income included either a worker, an unemployed job-seeker, or a retired worker. Almost half of the families included children; of those, 57% were headed by a single mother, 36% by two parents, and 6% by a single father. Looking at participants by age, the survey found that 37% of individuals served were children age 17 or younger, and 20% were seniors age 55 or older. More than 59% of individuals reported they were white and 26% were African American. Almost 18% of individuals reported their ethnicity as Hispanic or Latino, regardless of race.

The survey collected information on potential barriers to self-sufficiency and reported that, of people served by the CSBG network in FY2012, approximately 34% had no health insurance; 19% had disabilities; and 35% of participating adults older than 24 had no high school diploma or equivalency certificate.

# Funding and Legislative Proposals for FY2014[15]

## Interim Continuing Resolution

Congress has not yet passed any full-year appropriations bills for FY2014. A funding gap began on October 1, 2013 (the beginning of FY2014), and ended on October 17, 2013, with the enactment of an interim continuing resolution (CR) that provides budget authority for federal programs, including CSBG and related activities, through January 15, 2014 (P.L. 113-46). In general, the interim CR maintains programs at their FY2013 levels, including reductions that resulted from the March 1, 2013, budget "sequester" and an across-the-board rescission determined necessary by OMB to keep discretionary spending below statutory limits. (See **Table 1** for these reduced FY2013 amounts.) However, as of this writing, the FY2014 budget and appropriations process is still ongoing.

## Senate Committee Action on Full-Year Appropriations Bill

Although no further action has occurred on this bill, the Senate Appropriations Committee on July 11 reported legislation that would provide full-year FY2014 appropriations for the Departments of Labor, HHS, and Education (S. 1284, S.Rept. 113-71). As reported, the bill includes a total of $732 million for CSBG and related activities, broken down as follows: $676 million for the block grant, $30 million for CED, $6 million for RCF, and $20 million for IDAs. These amounts are similar to FY2012 levels, but include an increase of $1 million over FY2012 for RCF.

In its report, the Senate Appropriations Committee said it rejected the Administration's proposed cuts to CSBG (see below) and "continues to strongly support the program, which provides critical and flexible funding for local organizations that serve as a central source of assistance for low-income populations at the local level."[16] With regard to the Administration's proposal to eliminate CED and move funding for the Healthy Food Financing Initiative to the Treasury Department, the

---

[15] For background on FY2014 appropriations for HHS and related agencies, see CRS Report R43236, *Labor, Health and Human Services, and Education (L-HHS-ED): FY2014 Appropriations*, coordinated by Karen E. Lynch.

[16] S.Rept. 113-71, p. 137.

committee "strongly encourages" collaboration between HHS and Treasury but noted that HFFI projects funded through the two agencies are distinct from each other and recommended continued funding for the CED. The committee also adopted bill language requested by the Administration to allow the recapture and reallocation of unused funds in the IDA program.

## Administration Proposal

President Obama submitted his FY2014 budget request to Congress on April 10, 2013, proposing $350 million for the CSBG, $19.5 million for IDAs, and no funding for the other CSBG-related activities.[17] This request would cut block grant funding almost in half and was consistent with the Administration's request for CSBG in both FY2012 and FY2013; however, Congress rejected this proposal in each of those two years.

Along with its request for reduced funding, the Administration proposed targeting CSBG resources to "high-performing, innovative" agencies and repeated its previously-stated intention to work with Congress to develop a set of core federal standards that states would use to determine whether existing eligible entities are performing successfully. In the case of an eligible entity that failed to meet these federal standards (which could be augmented with standards established by the states, subject to federal approval), the state would be required immediately to conduct an open competition to designate another entity to serve the affected community. A similar proposal was included in the FY2013 budget proposal; for more details on the core federal standards, see discussion below in "Administration Proposal" for FY2013.

The Administration proposed no change in the current funding distribution formula to states, territories, and tribes, but wants to require states to allocate funds among local agencies with "increased consideration" to the areas of greatest need. The Administration also proposed to allow states to suspend and redistribute funds so that interim services can be provided to low-income communities in cases where there is evidence of criminal wrongdoing or gross negligence. Additional proposals included requiring states to establish minimum guidance for grantees to use in determining the income eligibility of recipients of direct services, and requiring eligible entities to include performance measures that are responsive to local community needs in their Community Action Plans. See **Table 1** for a comparison of FY2014 recommended funding levels for CSBG and related activities with previous years' appropriations.

# Funding and Legislative Proposals for FY2013[18]

## Final Continuing Resolution

CSBG and related activities were funded in FY2013 under a full-year CR in the absence of a regular appropriations bill for the Departments of Labor, HHS, Education and related agencies. The final full-year CR for FY2013 (P.L. 113-6) generally maintained discretionary programs at

---

[17] See Administration for Children and Families, Department of Health and Human Services (HHS), 2014 Justifications of Estimates for Appropriations Committees: https://www.acf hhs.gov/sites/default/files/olab/fy_2014_cj_final_web.pdf.

[18] For background on FY2013 appropriations for HHS and related agencies, see CRS Report R42588, *Labor, Health and Human Services, and Education: FY2013 Appropriations Overview* , coordinated by Karen E. Lynch.

their FY2012 levels. A CR for the first six months of FY2013 (P.L. 112-175) had funded these programs at their FY2012 levels, *plus* an additional 0.612%.

For CSBG and related activities, FY2012 levels were $677 million for CSBG, $30 million for CED (of which up to $10 million could be used for the Healthy Food Financing Initiative), $5 million for RCF, and $20 million for IDAs. For FY2013, however, these levels were reduced as a result of a sequestration ordered on March 1 and an across-the-board rescission that OMB determined was necessary to keep FY2013 discretionary spending within statutory limits. On May 20, HHS published an "all-purpose table" that shows a combined total of $687 million for CSBG and related activities in FY2013, including $635 million for the CSBG, $28 million for CED, $5 million for RCF, and almost $19 million for IDAs.

"Sequestration" is an automatic across-the-board spending reduction process under which budgetary resources are permanently canceled to enforce budget policy goals. Under the Budget Control Act of 2011 (P.L. 112-25), OMB was directed to implement automatic budget enforcement mechanisms, including sequestration, of FY2013-FY2021 funding to enforce certain deficit reduction goals. The FY2013 sequestration originally was scheduled to occur on January 2, 2013, but was postponed by the American Taxpayer Relief Act (P.L. 112-240). OMB ultimately issued the sequester order on March 1, announcing that nonexempt nondefense discretionary programs (such as CSBG and related activities) would be subject to a 5% reduction.[19]

OMB further announced on April 4, subsequent to the enactment of P.L. 113-6, that an across-the-board rescission of 0.2% was necessary to avoid a breach of statutory limits on discretionary spending for FY2013. The effect of these reductions on final amounts available in FY2013 for CSBG and related activities—resulting both from the March 1 sequester and from the across-the-board rescission—is reflected in the "all-purpose table" published by HHS on May 20, described above. (See **Table 1**).

## House Action on Full-Year Appropriations Bill in the 112th Congress

During the 112th Congress, the House Labor-HHS-Education Appropriations Subcommittee approved and released a draft FY2013 funding bill, which included $712 million for CSBG and related activities, plus an unspecified amount for IDAs.[20] In its recommendation for the block grant, the House subcommittee would have maintained funding at current levels and rejected the Administration's proposal to reduce block grant funding by approximately half. Specifically, the bill would have provided $677 million for the block grant; $30 million for CED; and $5 million for RCF. However, the draft bill would have prohibited any use of funds for the Administration's Healthy Food Financing Initiative. The full House Appropriations Committee did not act on this bill.

---

[19] See OMB Report to the Congress on the Joint Committee Sequestration for FY2013: http://www.whitehouse.gov/sites/default/files/omb/assets/legislative_reports/fy13ombjcsequestrationreport.pdf.

[20] A press release summarizing the House Subcommittee's draft bill, and the legislative text of the bill, can be found on the House Appropriations Committee website: http://appropriations.house.gov/news/documentsingle.aspx?DocumentID=303303.

## Senate Action on Full-Year Appropriations Bill in the 112th Congress

The Senate Appropriations Committee reported S. 3295, its version of the FY2013 appropriations bill for the Departments of Labor, HHS, and Education. That bill included a total of $733 million for CSBG and related activities, divided as follows: $677 million for the block grant; $30 million for CED (with up to $10 million available for the Healthy Food Financing Initiative); $6 million for RCF; and $20 million for IDAs.

In its report accompanying the FY2013 bill, the Senate committee expressed strong support for CSBG

> which provides critical flexible funding for local organizations that serve as a central source of assistance for low-income populations. These local organizations typically administer larger Federal programs such as Head Start and LIHEAP [Low-Income Home Energy Assistance Program]. The CSBG provides critical funding to support the administration of these programs at the local level, as well as flexible funding to fill in service gaps and meet the particular needs of local communities.[21]

## Administration Proposal

President Obama submitted his FY2013 budget request to Congress in February of 2012, proposing a total of almost $400 million for CSBG and related activities, compared to a final level of $732 million in FY2012. The block grant would have been reduced by nearly half (from $677 million to $350 million) and RCF (funded in FY2012 at $5 million) would have been eliminated. CED and IDAs would have remained at FY2012 levels (nearly $30 million and $20 million, respectively). Of funds provided for CED, $10 million were to go to the Administration's Healthy Food Financing Initiative.

Budget documents characterized the proposed reduction in funding for CSBG as one of several "tough cuts to worthy programs necessary to offset spending increases for other HHS programs."[22] In addition to cutting funding for CSBG, the Administration sought to increase quality and competition in the program and to focus resources on the highest-performing agencies. The FY2013 budget justifications repeated many of the same comments made in the FY2012 budget request (see FY2012 "Administration Proposal" below), noting that annual funding to local agencies is not competitive and that many of the same local agencies have been receiving funding through CSBG and its predecessor program since 1964.[23] While the law provides a mechanism for states to terminate funding for local agencies, the process "can be protracted," according to HHS.

HHS again noted that National Performance Indicators (NPIs) and a performance management system called Results Oriented Management Accountability (ROMA) are used to track performance and provide national accountability for the activities of local grantees. However, because the grantees receive funding from numerous sources in addition to CSBG, the

---

[21] See S.Rept. 112-176.

[22] FY2013 Budget of the United States, Office of Management and Budget, p. 108; http://www.gpo.gov/fdsys/pkg/BUDGET-2013-BUD/pdf/BUDGET-2013-BUD.pdf.

[23] See Administration for Children and Families, Department of Health and Human Services (HHS), 2013 Justifications of Estimates for Appropriations Committees, pp. 190-191; http://transition.acf.hhs.gov/sites/default/files/assets/CFS%20final.pdf.

performance accountability system cannot identify outcomes solely attributable to CSBG funding. Moreover, these performance data are not used to allocate funds among agencies.

The Administration proposed to work with Congress to develop a set of "core" federal standards that states would use to evaluate the performance of local eligible entities. States would also be able to augment these federal standards. If an eligible entity failed to meet the performance standards, the state would be required to hold an immediate open competition for another grantee to serve the affected community. At a minimum, the core standards would include the following criteria:

- failure to correct certain audit findings;

- board governance issues;

- failure to submit required financial, administrative, or programmatic reports and materials in a timely manner;

- failure to implement corrective actions based on state monitoring reviews for weakness in performance; and

- service delivery performance.

The Administration requested no change in the current law formula used to allocate CSBG funds among states, territories, and tribes. However, under the Administration proposals, states would be required to allocate funds among local agencies increasingly to "areas of greatest need."

No formal legislation was offered to implement any of the Administration's proposed changes to the CSBG program. However, the Administration contracted with the Urban Institute to facilitate the activities of a new CSBG Performance Management Task Force. These activities are described in a November 2012 letter from HHS.[24]

# Appropriations History: FY2009-FY2012

## FY2012[25]

### Final Congressional Action

During most of the first quarter of FY2012, CSBG and related activities—and many other government programs—operated under a series of continuing resolutions (CRs), which generally funded discretionary programs at FY2011 levels. On December 23, 2011, President Obama signed into law a full-year appropriations bill for FY2012 (P.L. 112-74), which maintained the block grant and RCF at approximately their FY2011 levels. P.L. 112-74 provided an increase for CED in FY2012, eliminated JOLI, and reduced spending for IDAs.

---

[24] This letter is available at http://www.acf.hhs.gov/programs/ocs/resource/csbg-performance-management-task-force-dear-colleague-letter. Also see a more detailed summary of performance management activities at http://www.acf.hhs.gov/programs/ocs/resource/csbg-fy-2013-update.

[25] For background on FY2012 appropriations for the Departments of Labor, HHS, and Education, see CRS Report R42010, *Labor, Health and Human Services, and Education: FY2012 Appropriations*, coordinated by Karen E. Lynch.

---

Specifically, the Consolidated Appropriations Act, 2012, provided $679 million for CSBG, which was the same level provided in FY2011. The law also provided $30 million for CED, which was up from $18 million in FY2011, but up to $10 million of the FY2012 appropriation could be used for the Healthy Foods Financing Initiative. The law included $5 million for RCF (same as FY2011); no funding for JOLI (which had received $1.6 million in FY2011); and $20 million for IDAs (down from $24 million in FY2011). All of the FY2012 amounts were subject to an across-the-board rescission of 0.198%, resulting in the slightly reduced amounts shown in **Table 1**.

## Administration Proposal

President Obama released his Administration's FY2012 budget on February 14, 2011, seeking a total of $394 million for CSBG and related activities.[26] Of this amount, $350 million would have gone to the block grant, for a reduction of 50% from FY2010 levels (or 48% from final FY2011 levels). The Administration's proposal to reduce funding for CSBG was coupled with a statement of intent to "inject competition" into the program. As described earlier, states are required under current law to pass at least 90% of their annual block grant allotments to "eligible entities," which are primarily Community Action Agencies that had been designated under the former Economic Opportunity Act of 1964. In FY2012 budget documents, HHS noted that these grants are not open for competition and that while states may terminate funding for CAAs that are found to be deficient, this process is seen as burdensome and is not pursued often. "States usually pursue termination only when there is a determination that the CAA is grossly financially negligent," according to HHS.

Office of Management and Budget (OMB) documents further stated: "A series of reports from the Government Accountability Office and the Inspector General of the Department of Health and Human Services have documented failures in program oversight and accountability—with the likely result that even grossly negligent CAAs continue to receive funding."[27]

In proposing a reduced funding level for FY2012, HHS stated:

> Within this reduced funding level, ACF will work with Congress to inject competition into the program so that resources are targeted more effectively on high-performing, innovative organizations. The program, as reconfigured, should maintain the current emphasis on place-based services to address the causes and impact of poverty, but should hold grantees more accountable for outcomes and should direct resources to agencies that can effectively serve high need communities, use evidence-based practice to achieve results, operate with a high level of program integrity, and maximize funding spent on services rather than administrative overhead. Many community action agencies deliver quality programs, but at a time when we must reduce the deficit, we cannot afford to provide guaranteed funding that is not targeted based on need and performance.

---

[26] Administration for Children and Families, Department of Health and Human Services (HHS), FY2012 Justification of Estimates for Appropriations Committees, Children and Families Services Programs, pp. 197-199, http://www.acf.hhs.gov/programs/olab/budget/2012/cj/CFS.pdf.

[27] Office of Management and Budget (OMB), Fiscal Year 2012 Terminations, Reductions, and Savings, p. 103, http://cdbapps/ksglibrary/2428_2012_TRS.pdf. Also see **Appendix B** of this report for a discussion of the GAO findings and recommendations referenced by OMB; and see Office of Inspector General, Department of Health and Human Services, *Alert: Community Service Block Grant Recovery Act Funding for Vulnerable and In-Crisis Community Action Agencies* (A-01-09-02511), http://oig.hhs.gov/oas/reports/region1/10902511.pdf.

---

Of the remaining budget request for CSBG and related activities in FY2012, CED would have received $20 million, down sharply from its FY2010 level of $36 million. (However, as noted below, the FY2012 request was actually higher than the final appropriation for FY2011, which provided $18 million for CED.) This program currently funds "an amalgam of projects with varying degrees of success," according to HHS budget documents. "In the most recent report to Congress, 21 percent of the projects funded were declared unsuccessful."[28] The Administration's request for CED would "trim available funding and better target resources to the Healthy Food Financing Initiative (HFFI), while at the same time, invigorate the program's competitive funding process."

Finally, the Administration proposed to maintain IDAs at their FY2011 level of $24 million in FY2012. No funding would have been provided for RCF or JOLI.

# FY2011

## Final Congressional Action

The 111th Congress failed to pass a regular FY2011 appropriations bill for the Departments of Labor, HHS, and Education. As a result, CSBG and related activities operated under a series of continuing resolutions (CRs) for the first half of the fiscal year. These temporary measures maintained CSBG and related activities at their FY2010 funding levels. A final CR for FY2011 (P.L. 112-10) was enacted on April 15, 2011, providing a total of $727 million for CSBG and related activities for the balance of the fiscal year; this amount was somewhat lower than the FY2010 level of $773 million.

P.L. 112-10 included a mandatory across-the-board rescission of 0.2% for discretionary non-defense programs. As implemented by HHS, final amounts provided under the law were $679 million for the block grant, $18 million for CED, and $5 million for RCF. Of funds provided for the block grant, the law required $350,000 to be used by the Secretary of HHS for preparation of a report on the use of CSBG funds. Final FY2011 funding levels for programs authorized outside the CSBG Act were $1.6 million for JOLI and $24 million for IDAs.

Earlier in the year, the House had passed alternative legislation (H.R. 1) to extend funding through the end of FY2011, which would have reduced discretionary funding for many government programs, including CSBG. As passed by the House on February 19, 2011, H.R. 1 contained $405 million for programs authorized under the CSBG Act, including $395 million for the block grant (compared with the FY2010 level of $700 million) and $10 million for RCF (which was the same as the FY2010 level). No funds would have been provided for CED, and JOLI and IDAs would have remained at their FY2010 funding levels of $2.6 million and $24 million, respectively.

During debate on H.R. 1, the House considered an amendment offered by Representative Flake that would have reduced FY2011 funding for the CSBG by an additional $100 million, which would have resulted in a total of $295 million for the block grant in FY2011. The amendment was defeated by a vote of 115 to 316.

---

[28] The most recent report to Congress posted on the HHS website is for FY2006: http://www.acf.hhs.gov/programs/ocs/ced/report/fy06/report_con.html.

On March 9, the Senate failed to pass the House version of H.R. 1 and also failed to pass S.Amdt. 149, which would have kept CSBG and related activities at their FY2010 levels through the balance of FY2011.[29]

## Administration Proposal

President Obama submitted a detailed FY2011 budget request to Congress on February 1, 2010, seeking a total of $760 million for CSBG and related activities ($700 million for the block grant, $36 million for CED, and $24 million for IDAs). In total, the request was lower than amounts provided in FY2010 because the Administration did not request funds in FY2011 for RCF or JOLI. Moreover, the Administration did not seek to continue the special $1 billion in funding provided to CSBG under the American Recovery and Reinvestment Act of 2009 (ARRA, P.L. 111-5). President Obama's budget request for FY2011 was similar to his request for FY2010, when he also proposed zero funding for RCF; however, the FY2010 request would have maintained level funding for JOLI.

Although the Administration proposed level funding ($36 million) for CED in FY2011, budget documents indicated that up to $20 million of this amount would be dedicated for use under the Healthy Food Financing Initiative.

HHS budget documents also indicated that the Office of Community Services planned to continue funding in FY2010 for a cooperative agreement grant for a national community economic development training and capacity development initiative; this grant began in FY2009 in response to directives from House and Senate Appropriations Committees.

# FY2010

With no final appropriations law in place at the beginning of FY2010, Congress passed a series of continuing resolutions to maintain funding for HHS and other federal agencies. The House and Senate subsequently passed the conference agreement on a full-year consolidated appropriations bill (H.R. 3288, H.Rept. 111-366), which was enacted on December 16, 2009, as P.L. 111-117.

The final law included the following amounts for CSBG and related activities: $700 million for the block grant, $36 million for CED, $10 million for RCF, $2.66 million for JOLI, and $24 million for IDAs. The Administration had originally requested $700 million for the block grant, $36 million for CED, $5.3 million for JOLI, and $24 million for IDAs. The Administration had proposed termination of RCF.

The conference agreement on the consolidated appropriations bill directed HHS to use $500,000 to continue the national training and capacity-building initiative that was started in FY2009, which the Administration said that it would. The agreement also directed HHS to report to the House and Senate Appropriations Committees on the use by states of the ARRA/CSBG funds intended for "benefit eligibility coordination" and whether these funds had achieved their

---

[29] For a comparison of proposed federal agency level funding in H.R. 1 and S.Amdt. 149, with FY2010 enacted levels and the Obama Administration's request for FY2011, see CRS Report R41703, *FY2011 Appropriations: A Side-by-Side Comparison of Key Proposals and Enacted Legislation*.

intended purpose of ensuring that individuals and families receive the assistance for which they are eligible under various federal, state, local, and private programs.

## American Recovery and Reinvestment Act of 2009[30]

On February 17, 2009, President Obama signed ARRA into law, providing an estimated $787 billion in spending and tax provisions in an effort to stimulate the economy.[31] The law appropriated $1 billion for the CSBG, which remained available for obligation until September 30, 2010. The funds were subject to set-aside provisions in the underlying CSBG law that reserved half of 1% for allocation among the territories and 1.5% for training, technical assistance, evaluation, and monitoring. Remaining funds were distributed according to the regular CSBG formula to states, which were required to use 1% of their ARRA allotments for "benefit eligibility coordination" activities, related to identification and enrollment of eligible individuals and families in federal, state, or local benefit programs. The balance of each state's allotment was distributed among local eligible entities in the state. ARRA provided that CSBG funds could be used in FY2009 and FY2010 to serve individuals and families with incomes up to 200% of the federal poverty level, rather than the regular CSBG maximum of 125% of poverty.

HHS issued formal guidance regarding the release and use of the CSBG stimulus funds on April 10, 2009, requiring states to submit a plan for use of the funds by May 29, 2009. In its guidance, HHS encouraged states and local entities that received stimulus funding to create "sustainable economic resources in communities."[32] Specifically, HHS said that states should help ensure that eligible entities

> 1) provide a wide range of innovative employment-related services and activities tailored to the specific needs of their community; 2) use funds in a manner that meets the short-term and long-term economic and employment needs of individuals, families and communities; and 3) make meaningful and measureable progress toward the reform goals of the Recovery Act with special attention to creating and sustaining economic growth and employment opportunities.

The guidance also noted that states could not use CSBG stimulus funds for administrative costs or any statewide discretionary activities.[33]

As noted above, states were required to use 1% of their CSBG allotments for coordination activities to ensure that eligible individuals were identified and enrolled in appropriate benefit

---

[30] For a summary of provisions in the economic stimulus legislation affecting CSBG and additional programs (Temporary Assistance for Needy Families, Child Care and Development Block Grant, Child Support Enforcement, Child Welfare, Low-Income Home Energy Assistance, Head Start, and the Compassion Capital Fund), see CRS Report R40211, *Human Services Provisions of the American Recovery and Reinvestment Act*.

[31] The Congressional Budget Office (CBO) subsequently re-estimated the amount of funding provided by ARRA and now estimates the law will result in spending of approximately $825 billion over the 10-year period of FY2009-FY2019; see *Estimated Impact of the American Recovery and Reinvestment Act on Employment and Economic Output from April 2011 through June 2011*, August 2011: http://www.cbo.gov/ftpdocs/123xx/doc12385/08-24-ARRA.pdf.

[32] Office of Community Services (OCS) Information Memorandum, Transmittal No. 109, dated 4/10/09: http://www.acf.hhs.gov/programs/ocs/csbg/guidance/im109 html. Also see "frequently asked questions" on ARRA CSBG funds: http://www.acf hhs.gov/programs/ocs/csbg/qna html; and a second version of "frequently asked questions": http://www.acf hhs.gov/programs/ocs/csbg/arra_questions htm.

[33] HHS has issued guidance on the liquidation and close-out of CSBG/ARRA funds; see OCS Information Memorandum, Transmittal No. 122, dated 12/3/10; http://www.acf.hhs.gov/programs/ocs/csbg/guidance/im122 html.

programs, and HHS said the law gave states flexibility in administering these coordination activities to best meet the needs of individuals, families, and communities. In the conference agreement on the FY2010 consolidated appropriations legislation, House and Senate conferees expressed concern that people affected by the recession are not receiving the various benefits and services for which they qualify and directed HHS to report to the House and Senate Appropriations Committees on states' use of these coordination funds and whether they achieved their intended purpose. According to the National Association of State Community Services Programs annual report cited earlier (see section headed "CSBG Program Data"), benefits coordination activities undertaken with ARRA funds included state and local agency "coordination with stakeholders, communication techniques, technological enhancements, and other initiatives." Specific examples included statewide data collection systems to allow various programs to share information, and statewide information campaigns to increase public awareness of available services.[34]

The final version of ARRA was a hybrid of provisions passed earlier by the House and the Senate. In explaining its decision to include CSBG funding in the stimulus package, the House Appropriations Committee's draft report on ARRA stated:

> Due to rising unemployment, housing foreclosures, and high food and fuel prices, community action agencies have seen dramatic increases in requests for assistance. These additional economic recovery funds will help to fill gaps in safety net services by targeting funds directly to community action agencies in over 1,000 local communities while they are impacted by revenue shortfalls.[35]

In the Senate, the Appropriations Committee explained its decision to require states to reserve funds for benefit eligibility coordination activities: "These services help stabilize families, especially during periods of unemployment, and provide them with the tools they need to lift themselves from poverty and to establish economic self-sufficiency" (S.Rept. 111-3).

## FY2009

Congress passed and President Obama signed into law an omnibus appropriations act (P.L. 111-8) that funded CSBG and related activities from March through the balance of FY2009. From the beginning of FY2009, CSBG and related agencies had been operating under a continuing resolution (P.L. 110-329) that generally maintained funding at FY2008 levels. For CSBG and related agencies, the omnibus appropriations act for FY2009 provided a total of $775 million—as originally recommended by the House Labor-HHS-Education Appropriations Subcommittee— compared to total FY2008 funding of $722 million.

The House Labor-HHS-Education Appropriations Subcommittee had approved legislation on June 19, 2008, that would have increased funds for CSBG and two related activities in FY2009. The full House Appropriations Committee met but did not complete action on this bill on June 26, 2008. As approved by the subcommittee, the measure included $700 million for the CSBG (a $46

---

[34] HHS provided funding to the Urban Institute to evaluate ARRA-funded CSBG activities. A summary of the Urban Institute findings is available at http://www.spotlightonpoverty.org/ExclusiveCommentary.aspx?id=63653882-4051-41f4-afcc-600db45ab7b2. The full Urban Institute report, published in February 2012, is available at http://www.urban.org/UploadedPDF/412602-Implementation-of-Community-Services-Block-Grants-under-ARRA.pdf.

[35] The Committee's report is available on its website, http://appropriations.house.gov/images/stories/pdf/ RecoveryReport01-15-09.pdf.

million increase from the FY2008 level), $36 million for CED (a $4.5 million increase), $10 million for RCF (a $2.1 million increase), and level funding for JOLI and IDAs. The draft committee report stated that "the CSBG is more important than ever, with unemployment and poverty increasing due to the struggling economy and the number of low-income individuals and families in need of assistance rising as a consequence."[36] The draft report directed that $500,000 of training and technical assistance funds be used for a national community economic development training and capacity development initiative that would provide CAA leaders with the necessary professional skills to finance and implement innovative housing, economic, and community development partnerships. This language also was included in the explanatory statement accompanying P.L. 111-8.

The Senate Appropriations Committee reported its version of the FY2009 funding bill for the Departments of Labor, HHS, and Education on July 8, 2008 (S. 3230, S.Rept. 110-410). The Senate committee would have maintained CSBG and all related activities at their FY2008 funding levels, except for RCF, which would have received $8.5 million (a $600,000 increase). The Senate committee noted "the importance of Community Action Agencies (CAAs) as institutions that organize low-income communities to identify emerging challenges to economically insecure Americans and subsequently to mobilize the resources, programs and partnerships needed to address local poverty conditions." The report further stated that "CSBG is a unique Federal resource that supports CAAs while they initiate creative responses to local poverty conditions and seek new sources of support and investment to implement their initiatives. The committee believes that CSBG funding is an investment, analogous to venture capital, in the future of low-wage workers, retirees and their families."

In its report, the Senate committee faulted the Office of Community Services within HHS for failing to report on progress made in correcting the deficiencies in program oversight identified by the Government Accountability Office (GAO) (see **Appendix B** for a discussion of the GAO report). The committee further stated that OCS should develop and deliver professional skills training for CAA leaders so they can finance and implement innovative housing, economic, and community development partnerships (similar to language in the draft House report); that OCS should support linkages between local agencies, national organizations, and academic institutions that would disseminate research on effective responses to poverty; and finally, that OCS should continue funding statewide CAA associations to continue and expand cost-effective training and other capacity-building services for members. These concerns were repeated by the House Appropriations Committee in its explanatory statement accompanying the FY2009 omnibus appropriations bill that was enacted as P.L. 111-8. As noted above, HHS began funding the national training and capacity-building initiative in FY2009.

---

[36] Unnumbered draft House Appropriations Committee report, reflecting actions of the Subcommittee on Labor-HHS-Education on FY2009 spending bill, http://www.cq.com/flatfiles/editorialFiles/budgetTracker/reference/docs/20080626lhreport.pdf.

## Table 1. Funding for CSBG and Related Activities, FY2008-FY2014

($ in millions)

| Program | FY2008[a] | FY2009[b] | FY2010 | FY2011[c] | FY2012[d] | FY2013 CR[e] | FY2014 Request | FY2014 Senate[f] |
|---|---|---|---|---|---|---|---|---|
| Community Services Block Grant | 653.80 | 700.00 | 700.00 | 678.64 | 677.36 | 635.28 | 350.00 | 676.00 |
| Community Economic Development | 31.47 | 36.00 | 36.00 | 17.96 | 29.94 | 28.08 | 0 | 29.88 |
| Job Opportunities for Low-Income Individuals (JOLI) | 5.29 | 5.29 | 2.64 | 1.64 | 0 | 0 | 0 | 0 |
| Rural Community Facilities | 7.86 | 10.00 | 10.00 | 4.99 | 4.98 | 4.67 | 0 | 5.97 |
| Individual Development Accounts | 24.02 | 24.02 | 23.91 | 23.98 | 19.87 | 18.59 | 19.47 | 20.00 |
| **Total** | **722.45** | **775.31**[b] | **772.55** | **727.21** | **732.15** | **686.63** | **369.47** | **731.86** |

**Source:** Prepared by the Congressional Research Service (CRS). Unless otherwise noted, sources of data are agency budget justifications and congressional appropriations documents.

**Note:** Of amounts shown for Community Economic Development (CED) in FY2012 and FY2013, up to $10 million could be used for the Healthy Food Financing Initiative (HFFI). The Senate bill for FY2014 also assumed spending for HFFI as part of CED.

a. Funding reflects a 1.747% across-the-board reduction, as mandated by the Consolidated Appropriations Act, 2008 (P.L. 110-161).

b. Funding levels shown for FY2009 were included in P.L. 111-8 and do not include the additional $1 billion provided to the CSBG under the American Recovery and Reinvestment Act (ARRA, P.L. 111-5).

c. Funding reflects a 0.2% across-the-board rescission as mandated by P.L. 112-10.

d. The Consolidated Appropriations Act, 2012 (P.L. 112-74) mandated that appropriated amounts were subject to an across-the-board rescission of 0.189%. Amounts shown in this table reflect that rescission, as implemented by HHS and displayed in the FY2013 justifications for the Administration for Children and Families.

e. The source for numbers shown in this column is the "all-purpose table" published by the Administration for Children and Families at HHS on May 20, 2013. Numbers shown reflect the effects of budget sequestration and an across-the-board rescission of 0.2%. Under the terms of the interim continuing resolution for FY2014 enacted on October 17, 2013, these amounts remain in effect through January 15, 2014 (P.L. 113-46).

f. S. 1284, reported by the Senate Appropriations Committee on July 11, 2013.

### Table 2. Community Services Block Grant Appropriations History, FY1982-FY2013

($ in millions)

| Fiscal Year | Appropriation | Fiscal Year | Appropriation |
|---|---|---|---|
| FY1982 | 315 | FY1998 | 490 |
| FY1983 | 342 | FY1999 | 500 |
| FY1984 | 317 | FY2000 | 528 |
| FY1985 | 335 | FY2001 | 600 |
| FY1986 | 321 | FY2002 | 650 |
| FY1987 | 335 | FY2003 | 646 |
| FY1988 | 326 | FY2004 | 642 |
| FY1989 | 319 | FY2005 | 637 |
| FY1990 | 322 | FY2006 | 630 |
| FY1991 | 349 | FY2007 | 630 |
| FY1992 | 360 | FY2008 | 654 |
| FY1993 | 372 | FY2009 | 700 |
| FY1994 | 397 | FY2010 | 700 |
| FY1995 | 390 | FY2011 | 679 |
| FY1996 | 390 | FY2012 | 677 |
| FY1997 | 490 | FY2013 | 635 |

**Source:** Prepared by the Congressional Research Service (CRS), based on information in Department of Health and Human Services congressional budget justifications.

**Notes:** In addition to amounts shown for FY2009 and FY2010, the American Recovery and Reinvestment Act (ARRA, P.L. 111-5) included a one-time appropriation of $1 billion for CSBG, to be available for obligation in those two years.

# Appendix A. Reauthorization Attempts

The authorizing legislation for CSBG and related activities expired at the end of FY2003 but Congress has continued funding these activities nonetheless. No reauthorizing legislation has been introduced since the 109th Congress. The following discusses legislation considered in the 109th and 108th Congresses, as background information for any reauthorization discussions that may occur in the future.

In the 109th Congress, Representative Osborne introduced H.R. 341, the Improving the Community Services Block Grant Act, which was virtually identical (except for dates) to legislation passed by the House during the 108th Congress (H.R. 3030).[37] H.R. 341 would have reauthorized the CSBG and related activities through FY2012, and was referred to the House Education and the Workforce Committee, where no action occurred. In his introductory remarks, Representative Osborne noted key provisions of H.R. 341, such as promoting increased quality and accountability of CSBG programs, encouraging initiatives to improve conditions and eliminate barriers to self-sufficiency in rural areas, and providing youth mentoring services to address education needs and crime.

Other provisions of H.R. 341 would have

- changed the definition of the "eligible entity" by requiring such entities to establish and meet local goals as well as state goals, standards, and requirements;

- required that a state take swift action to improve the performance or terminate funding of low-performing eligible entities or ones that failed to meet local and state requirements;

- provided that a state justify to the Secretary its continued support of low-performing eligible entities;

- required a state to use funds to improve economic conditions and remove barriers to self-sufficiency for the rural poor;

- required a local eligible entity to establish goals for reducing poverty in the community;

- based subsequent grant awards on the success or failure of an eligible entity in meeting goals;

- prohibited a religious organization providing services under provisions of this act from discriminating against a person seeking assistance because of religion or a religious belief;

- required the Secretary to establish procedures that would allow grant funds or intangible assets acquired with grant funds to become the sole property of the grantee if the grantee agrees to continue to use the funds or property for the purposes for which the grant was provided;

- added water and wastewater facility needs to activities allowed for rural community development; and

---

[37] H.R. 3030 contained an unrelated unemployment compensation provision, which was not included in H.R. 341.

- added improvement of academic achievement to the goals of national or regional programs designed to provide instruction activities.

During the 108th Congress, the committee reported and the House passed H.R. 3030 (virtually identical to H.R. 341 in the 109th Congress), while the Senate passed S. 1786, the Poverty Reduction and Prevention Act. Conferees never met to resolve differences in the two bills. Both bills in the 108th Congress would have reauthorized CSBG and related programs at such sums as necessary, except for the National Youth Sports Program, which would have been reauthorized at $15 million annually by the House bill and $18 million by the Senate bill. The following compares provisions of H.R. 3030 and S. 1786 from the 108th Congress; readers should note that H.R. 341, introduced in the 109th Congress, contained the same provisions as H.R. 3030.

## Program Goals

H.R. 3030 and S. 1786 contained similar provisions concerning goals of eligible entities. H.R. 3030 would have required entities to establish and meet locally determined goals for reducing poverty in the community. It would also have added "improving academic achievement" to the list of required goals. Both bills would have required an entity to include goals for leveraging community resources; fostering coordination of federal, state, local, private, and other assistance; and promoting community involvement.

S. 1786 would have provided that grants to states support both improving the causes of poverty and the conditions that cause poverty. The measure would have revised the poverty line determination; it would have allowed a state to raise its eligibility threshold to a minimum of 125% of the federal poverty line or a maximum of 60% of state median income; however, the state would have had to give priority to serving individuals with the lowest income who sought services. Also, S. 1786 would have made a tripartite board the sole mechanism for determining consideration of eligible entities, and thus would have eliminated current provisions that allow a state to specify another mechanism for doing so. H.R. 3030 did not contain provisions concerning the poverty eligibility threshold or the role of a tripartite board in determining an eligible entity.

## State Plan Requirements

H.R. 3030 and S. 1786 would have revised state application and plan requirements. H.R. 3030 would have specified that youth development activities may include mentoring programs. The bill also would have added, as a use of funds to be included in the state plan, "initiatives to improve economic conditions and mobilize new resources in rural areas to eliminate obstacles to the self-sufficiency of families and individuals in rural communities." S. 1786 would have revised the current state plan provisions by requiring not only that the Secretary review the plan but also approve it. Among information for inclusion in a state's plan submitted to the Secretary was an assurance that grant funds would be used for the following purposes: to improve literacy, communications, and technical skills of participant low-income families; for initiatives to assist those moving from welfare to work to obtain jobs at decent wages with benefits; for initiatives to increase the development of household assets of individuals (such as individual development accounts and home-ownership opportunities); to improve economic conditions and mobilize new resources in rural and other at-risk areas to eliminate obstacles to the self-sufficiency of persons in those communities, and for initiatives to reduce the concentration of poverty in cities and inner suburbs and provide economic opportunities for persons in those areas; and in support of partnerships with nonprofit or community-based organizations that address child abuse prevention, including programs that are school-based and that focus on adolescent victims, and victimizers.

## Training and Technical Assistance

Both bills contained training and technical assistance provisions. H.R. 3030 would have added "dissemination regarding best practices" to the use of funds by the Secretary. S. 1786 would have revised training and technical assistance provisions by devising, in consultation with national and state networks of eligible entities, a strategic plan for annual technical assistance; and would have improved management information and reporting systems by developing a common state financial and organizational protocol.

## Grantee Funding Reduction or Termination

Provisions relating to reducing or terminating funding for eligible entities were included in H.R. 3030 and S. 1786. H.R. 3030 would have allowed, but not required, the Secretary to review determinations by a state to reduce or terminate funding to an eligible entity. Further, the bill would have amended the definition of "cause" in the case of a funding reduction to include failure to meet poverty reduction goals. States would have been required to give priority to entities that received funding on the date of enactment, if they fulfilled their poverty reduction goals. If no entity was entitled to such priority, the state would designate another entity from qualified applicants. H.R. 3030 also would have required states to replace the lowest performing existing grantees beginning in FY2005. S. 1786 would have established procedures for termination of designation as an eligible entity or reduction of funding by giving eligible entities a right to a public hearing on a state decision; changing from 90 to 30 days the time frame within which the Secretary must have made a determination concerning a state's decision to terminate or to reduce funding for an eligible entity; and requiring the Secretary to continue funding the entity at its previous year's level until a decision was made on a state's action.

## Grantee Monitoring and Fiscal Controls

Both measures would have amended current provisions of the CSBG Act relating to monitoring eligible entities. H.R. 3030 would have required federal reviews to determine whether local performance goals were being met. S. 1786 would have changed current law requirements for full on-site federal reviews of eligible entities every three years to a biennial basis. In addition, S. 1786 would have required an annual follow-up visit to entities that failed to meet state-established goals.

S. 1786 would have addressed fiscal controls by requiring states to submit a separate audit of CSBG funds to the Secretary covering disbursements to eligible entities, use of state administrative funds, and disbursement of state discretionary funds; H.R. 3030 contained no such provisions. S. 1786 would have authorized the Secretary to withhold administrative funds from states that were not in compliance with the CSBG Act and provide funds directly to the eligible entities. H.R. 3030 and S. 1786 would have provided that funding be directed at improving the self-sufficiency of families and individuals in rural communities.

Both H.R. 3030 and S. 1786 contained similar provisions that would have authorized the Secretary to allow grantees to keep assets obtained with program funds. H.R. 3030 would have allowed the Secretary to add water and waste water treatment to the list of community facility needs. H.R. 3030 would have allowed funds to be used for construction or substantial rehabilitation of buildings and facilities and for loans or investments in private business enterprises owned by community development corporations. S. 1786 would have authorized the Secretary to allow funds for long-term loans or investments for private business enterprises, capital to businesses owned by community development corporations, and marketing and management assistance for businesses providing jobs and business opportunities to low-income individuals.

## Faith-Based Organizations

Another key provision of H.R. 3030 and S. 1786 related to the participation of faith-based organizations in CSBG-funded programs. H.R. 3030 would have prohibited discrimination against a beneficiary or potential beneficiary of the program on the basis of religion. S. 1786 would have added religion to current provisions of the CSBG Act that prohibit exclusion of a person from program participation based on color, national origin, sex, or age. S. 1786 also would have amended current law, which requires government agencies to consider participation of religious organizations on the same basis as other nongovernmental organizations, to require religious organizations to meet requirements of the act.

There was debate on H.R. 3030 both in the House Committee on Education and the Workforce and on the House floor on provisions in current law that allow a religious organization to discriminate in hiring. The committee defeated an amendment that would have prevented a grantee from using religion as a basis for discriminating against a job applicant and agreed to one that would have prohibited a religious organization from using religion or a religious belief as a basis for discriminating against a person *seeking program services*.

After considering a number of amendments, the House passed H.R. 3030 on February 4, 2004. The House rejected H.Amdt. 459 (Woolsey) in the nature of a substitute that would have prohibited organizations from using CSBG funds to discriminate in hiring on the basis of religion. The House rejected both H.Amdt. 460 (Robert Scott) which would have required organizations to separate their religious services or activities from programs that used CSBG funds and H.Amdt. 461 (Robert Scott) which would have prohibited the use of federal CSBG funds to discriminate in hiring based on religion.

# Appendix B. Government Accountability Office (GAO) Review

The Government Accountability Office (GAO) released a report on the CSBG program in July 2006, which was originally requested by the House Education and the Workforce Committee in April 2005. GAO's review focused on three topics related to program monitoring and training and technical assistance: (1) HHS compliance with legal requirements and standards governing its oversight of state efforts to monitor local CSBG grantees; (2) efforts by states to monitor local grantee compliance with fiscal requirements and performance standards; and (3) targeting by HHS of its training and technical assistance funds and the impact of such assistance on grantee performance.[38]

GAO concluded that the Office of Community Services (OCS, the office within HHS that is charged with administering the CSBG) "lacks effective policies, procedures, and controls" to ensure its own compliance with legal requirements for monitoring states and with federal internal control standards. GAO found that OCS had visited states as mandated by law but failed to issue reports to the states after the visits or annual reports to Congress, which also are mandated by law. OCS failed to meet internal control standards because their monitoring teams lacked adequate financial expertise; moreover, OCS lost the documentation from the monitoring visits to states. Finally, OCS was not systematic in its selection of states to visit, and did not use available information on state performance or collect other data to allow more effective targeting of its limited monitoring resources on states at highest risk of management problems.

In connection with its assessment of state efforts to monitor local grantees, GAO visited five states and found wide variation in the frequency with which they conducted on-site monitoring of local grantees, although officials in all states said they visited agencies with identified problems more often. States also varied in their interpretation of the law's requirement that they visit local grantees at least once in a three-year period, and GAO noted that OCS had issued no guidance on this requirement. States reported varying capacities to conduct on-site monitoring and some states cited staff shortages; however, the states all performed other forms of oversight in addition to on-site visits, such as review of local agency reports (e.g., local agency plans, goals, performance data, and financial reports) and review of annual Single Audits where relevant. Several states coordinated local oversight with other federal and state programs, and also used state associations of Community Action Agencies to help provide technical assistance.

GAO found, with regard to federal training and technical assistance funds, that OCS targeted at least some of these funds toward local agencies with identified financial and program management problems, but generally was not strategic in allocating these funds and had only limited information on the outcome of providing such training and technical assistance.

---

[38] *Community Services Block Grant Program: HHS Should Improve Oversight by Focusing Monitoring and Assistance Efforts on Areas of High Risk*, GAO-06-627, U.S. Government Accountability Office, June 2006. GAO had revealed some of the findings of this review in February 2006 in a letter submitted to HHS ("Community Services Block Grant Program: HHS Needs to Improve Monitoring of State Grantees," GAO-06-373R, letter to Wade F. Horn, Assistant Secretary for Children and Families, Department of Health and Human Services, from the U.S. Government Accountability Office, February 7, 2006).

---

GAO made five recommendations to OCS in its report (and HHS indicated its agreement and intent to act upon these recommendations). According to GAO, OCS should

- conduct a risk-based assessment of states by systematically collecting and using information;

- establish policies and procedures to ensure monitoring is focused on the highest-risk states;

- issue guidance to states on complying with the requirement that they monitor local agencies during each three-year period;

- establish reporting guidance for training and technical assistance grants so that OCS receives information on the outcomes for local agencies that receive such training or technical assistance; and

- implement a strategic plan for targeting training and technical assistance in areas where states feel the greatest need.

## HHS Response

HHS took a series of steps in response to the GAO report. On October 10, 2006, HHS issued an information memorandum to state agencies responding to GAO's third recommendation and providing guidance on compliance with the statutory requirement that states conduct a full on-site review of each eligible entity at least once during every three-year period.[39] Subsequently, on March 1, 2007, HHS issued another information memorandum, responding to GAO's first two recommendations and providing a schedule of states that will receive federal monitoring in each of the next three years (FY2007-FY2009).[40]

The October memorandum explained that states were selected through a process intended to identify states that would receive the most benefit from federal monitoring visits. This process considered the extent to which eligible entities in the state were considered vulnerable or in crisis; the physical size of the state, its number of eligible entities, and the number of state personnel assigned to the CSBG program; the extent of poverty in the state compared to the number of eligible entities and state CSBG personnel; the number of clients served compared to the number of eligible entities and state CSBG personnel; evidence of past audit problems; and tardiness by the state in submitting CSBG state plans to HHS or responses to information surveys conducted by the National Association of State Community Services Programs.[41]

HHS developed a CSBG state assessment tool to help states prepare for federal monitoring,[42] and on August 24, 2007, issued a strategic plan for the CSBG program, which is intended to describe

---

[39] Office of Community Services (OCS) Information Memorandum, Transmittal No. 97, dated 10/10/06: http://www.acf.hhs.gov/programs/ocs/resource/im-no-97-guidance-on-the-csbg-requirement-to-monitor-eligible-entities.

[40] Office of Community Services (OCS) Information Memorandum, Transmittal No. 98, dated 3/1/07: http://www.acf.hhs.gov/programs/ocs/resource/im-no-1. The most recent monitoring schedule was provided in OCS Information Memorandum Transmittal No. 117, dated August 25, 2010, and covers FY2011-FY2013: http://www.acf.hhs.gov/programs/ocs/resource/no-117-three-year-csbg-monitoring-schedule-ffy-2011-ffy-2013.

[41] See discussion of this survey earlier in this report.

[42] Office of Community Services (OCS) Information Memorandum, Transmittal No. 102: http://www.acf.hhs.gov/sites/default/files/ocs/im_no_102_csbg_monitoring_checklist.pdf.

training, technical assistance, and capacity-building activities and promote accountability within the CSBG.[43] As discussed in the "Appropriations History" section of this report, HHS began funding the national community economic development training and capacity development initiative in FY2009. Most recently, HHS issued an information memorandum on May 4, 2011, announcing a reorganization and new "strategy for excellence" in the CSBG training and technical assistance program for FY2011.[44]

# Author Contact Information

Karen Spar
Specialist in Domestic Social Policy and Division
Research Coordinator
kspar@crs.loc.gov, 7-7319

---

[43] Office of Community Services (OCS) Information Memorandum, Transmittal No. 103, dated 8/24/07: http://www.acf.hhs.gov/sites/default/files/ocs/im_no_103_csbg_strategic_plan_final_strategic_plan.pdf.

[44] Office of Community Services (OCS) Information Memorandum, Transmittal No. 123, dated 5/4/11: http://www.acf.hhs.gov/programs/ocs/resource/reorganization-of-csbg-t-ta-resources-a-new-strategy-for-excellence.